Table of Contents

I0644073

Rourke Educational Media
rourkeeducationalmedia.com

Can you find these words?

colony

larvae

nest

queen

Amazing Ants

Ants live in groups.
Each group is called a **colony.**

Each ant has a job to do in the colony.

Worker ants build the **nest**.

Some ants find food for the colony.

They share the food with the other ants.

Some ants keep the nest safe.

One ant is **queen**. She lays eggs.

The other ants care for the babies. The babies are called **larvae**.

Ants work hard.

The colony is a team!

Did you find these words?

Each group is called a **colony.**

The babies are called **larvae.**

Worker ants build the **nest.**

One ant is **queen.**

Photo Glossary

colony (KAH-luh-nee): A group of animals that live together.

larvae (LAHR-vee): Insects at the stage of development after they hatch from eggs.

nest (nest): A place built by small creatures to live in and take care of their babies.

queen (kween): A female bee, wasp, or ant that can lay eggs.

Index

About the Author

Tammy Brown writes books and teaches teachers how to teach their students to read. She enjoys walking in the woods and watching little creatures like ants.

www.rourkeeducationalmedia.com

PHOTO CREDITS: Cover: ©RooM the Agency/©Alamy Stock Photo p. 2,3,14,15: ©Meister Photos; p. 2,10,14,15: ©Pavel Krasensky; p. 2,5,14,15: ©imageBROKER/©Alamy Stock Photo; p. 4: ©Pitamaha/©Alamy Stock Photo; p. 6: ©ChaiyaTN; p. 8: ©Henrik_L; p. 12: ©Tan Hung Meng

Edited by: Keli Sipperley
Cover and interior design by: Rhea Magaro-Wallace

Library of Congress PCN Data
Amazing Ants / Tammy Brown
(Plants, Animals, and People)
ISBN (hard cover)(alk. paper) 978-1-64156-156-3
ISBN (soft cover) 978-1-64156-212-6
ISBN (e-Book) 978-1-64156-267-6
Library of Congress Control Number: 2017957768

Printed in the United States of America, North Mankato, Minnesota